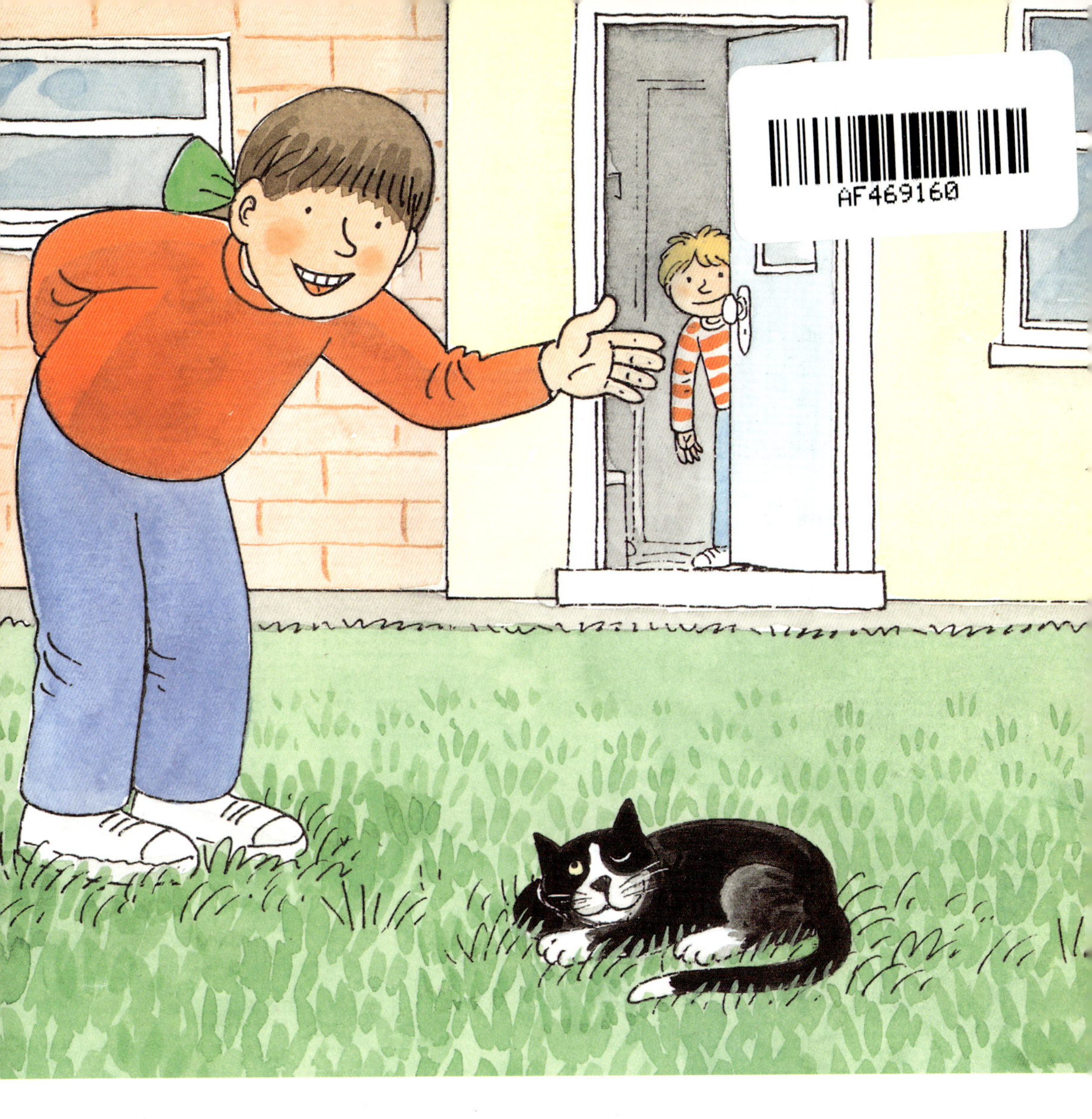

Go away, little cat.

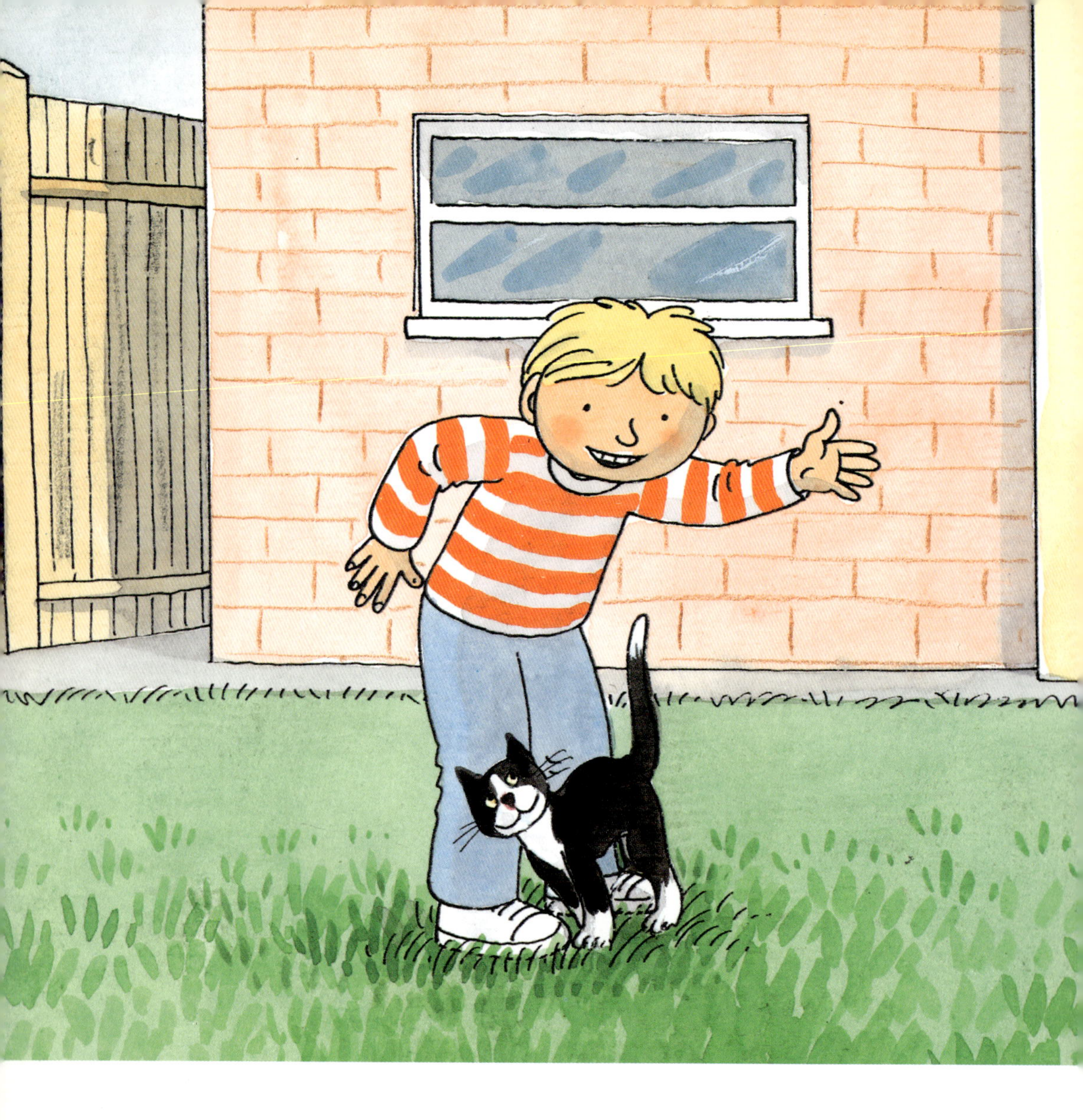

Go away, little cat.

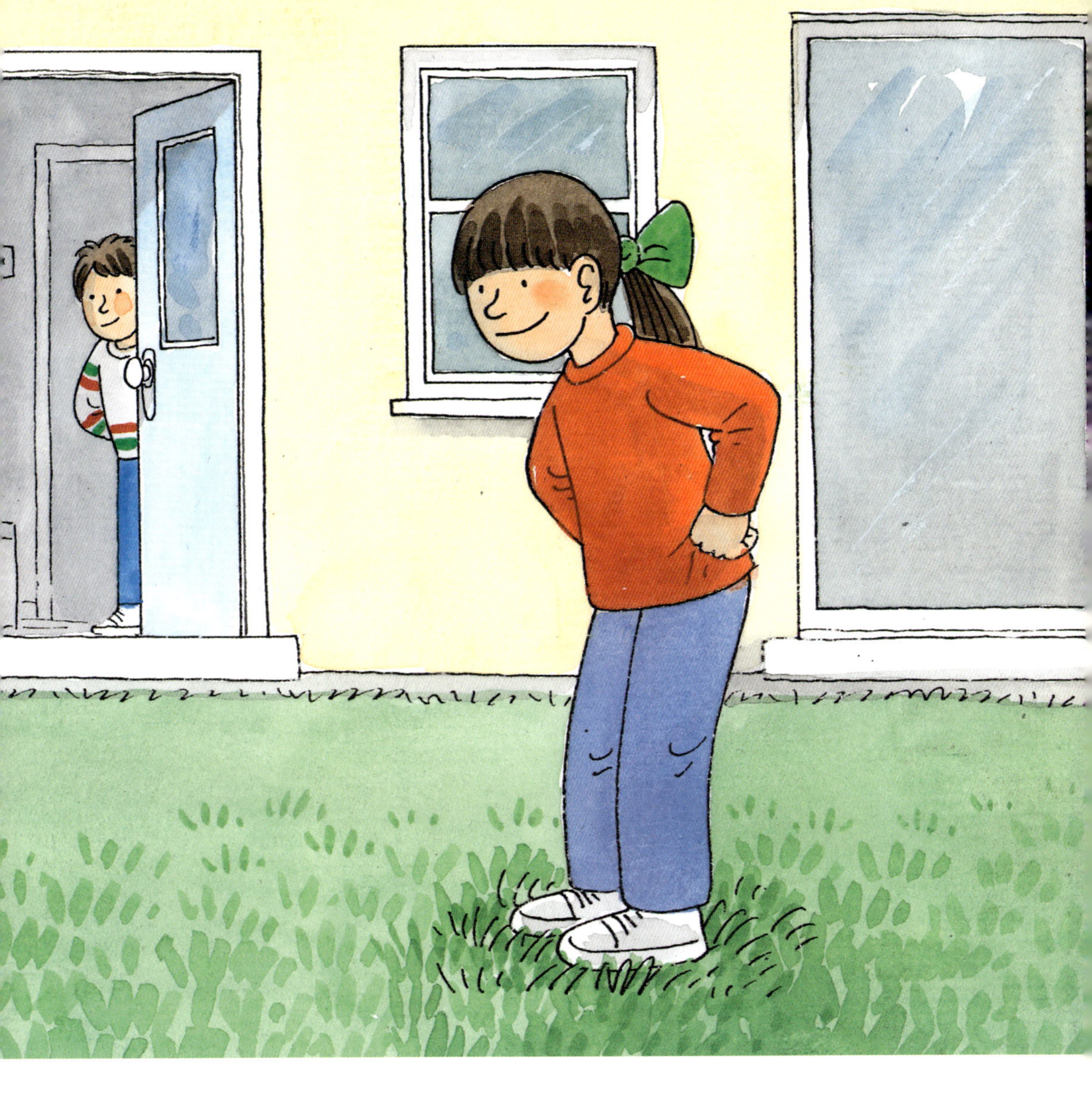

A dog is coming.

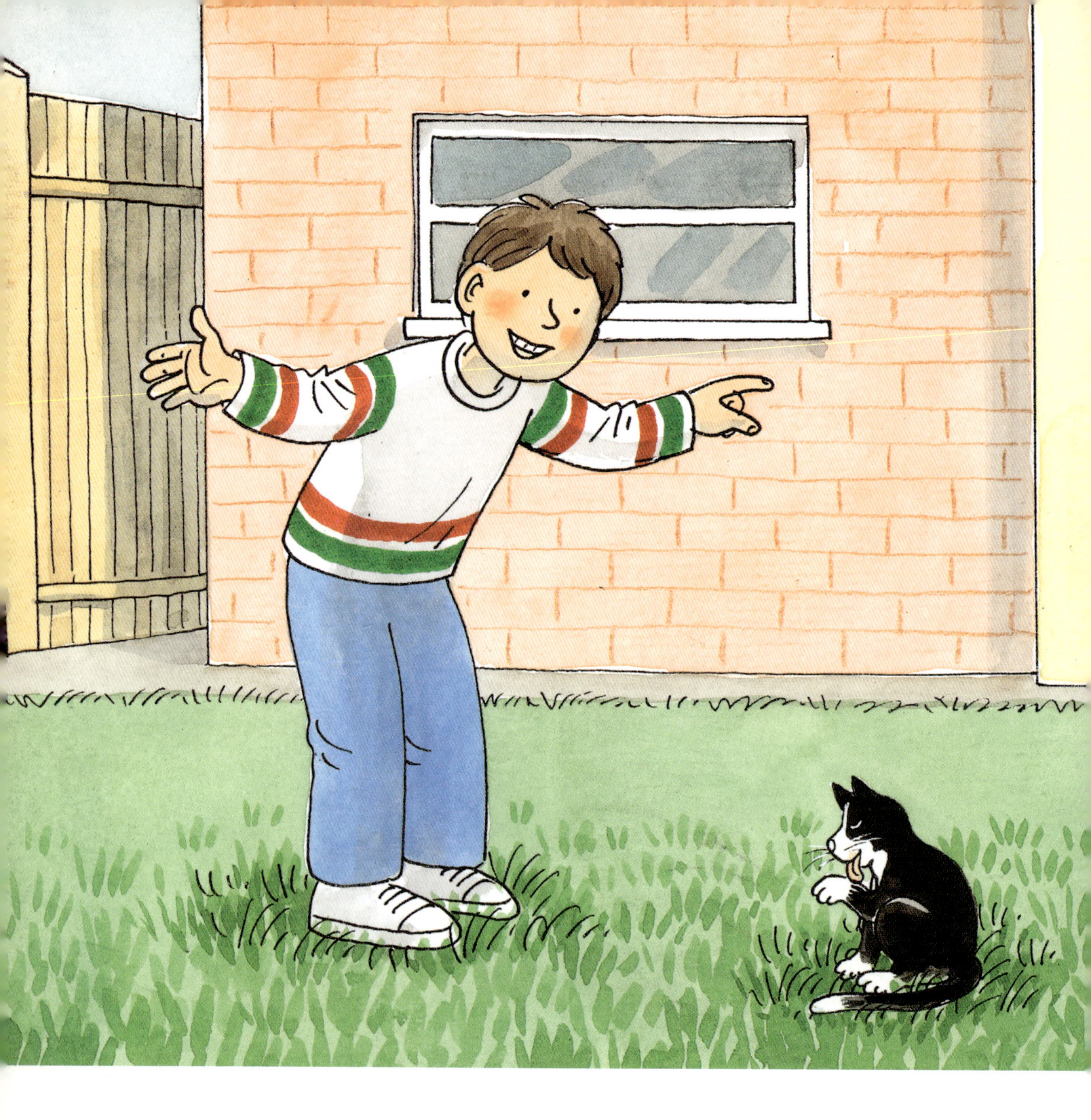

Go away, little cat.

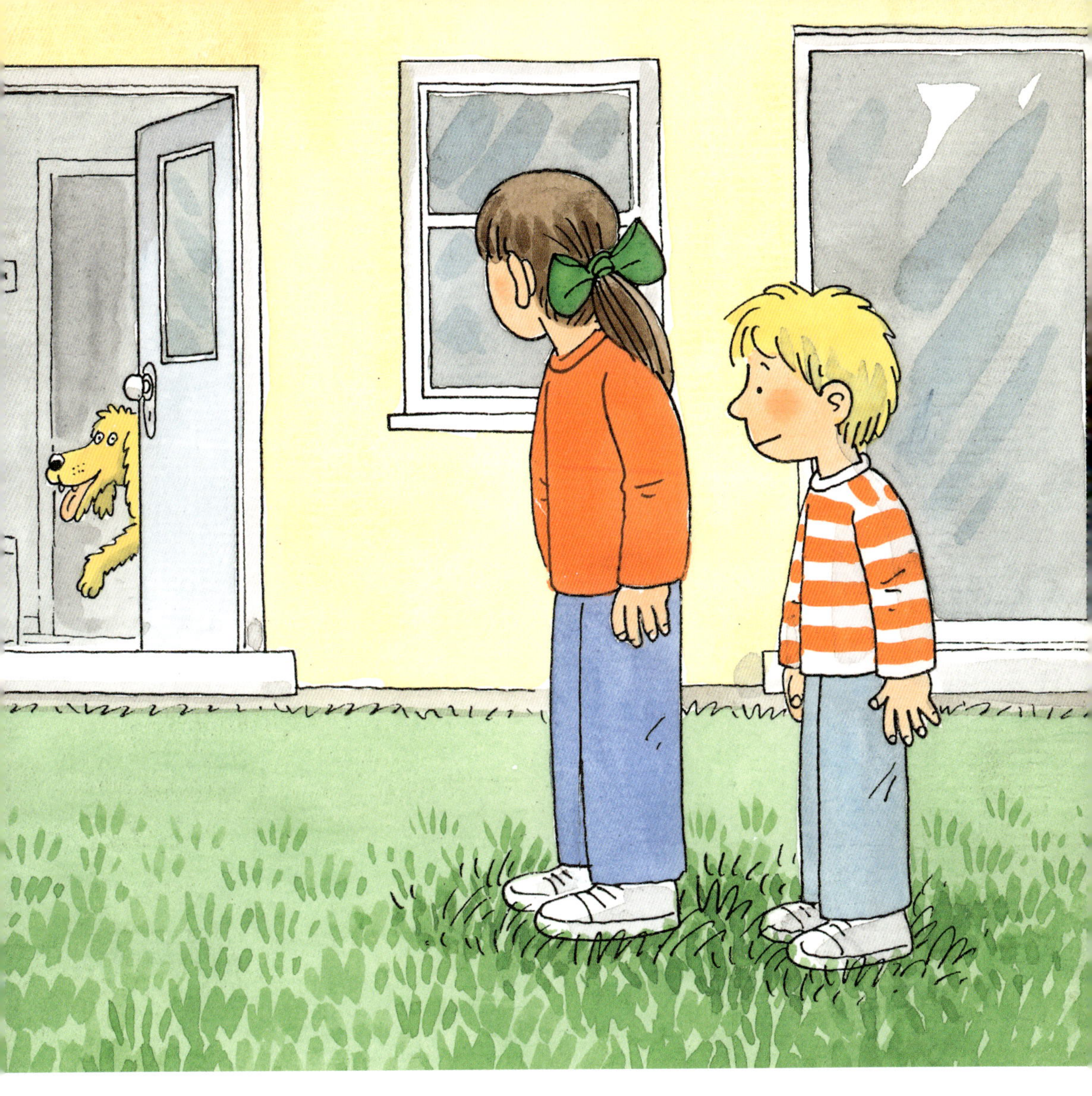

A big dog is coming.

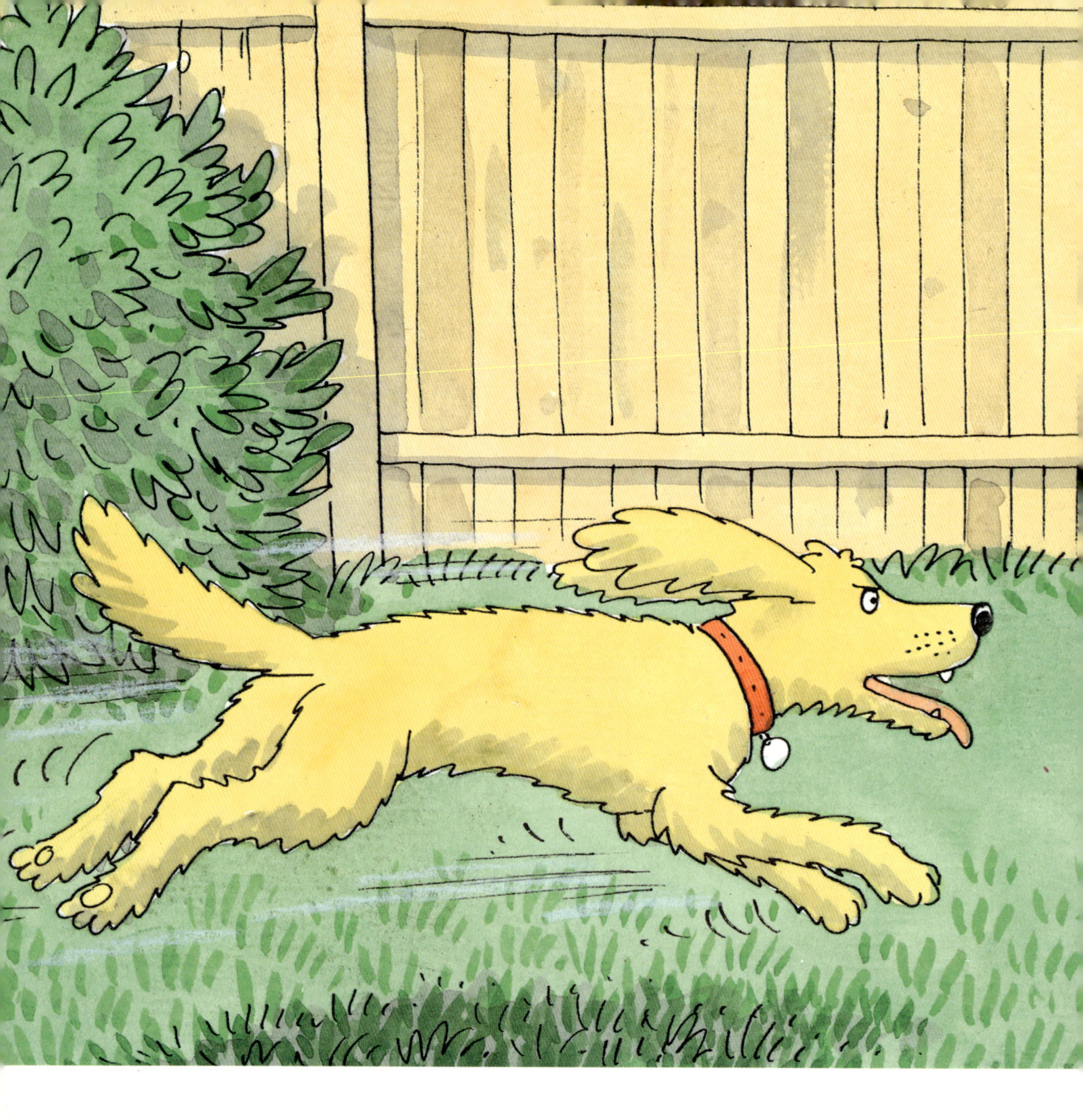

Go away, little cat.

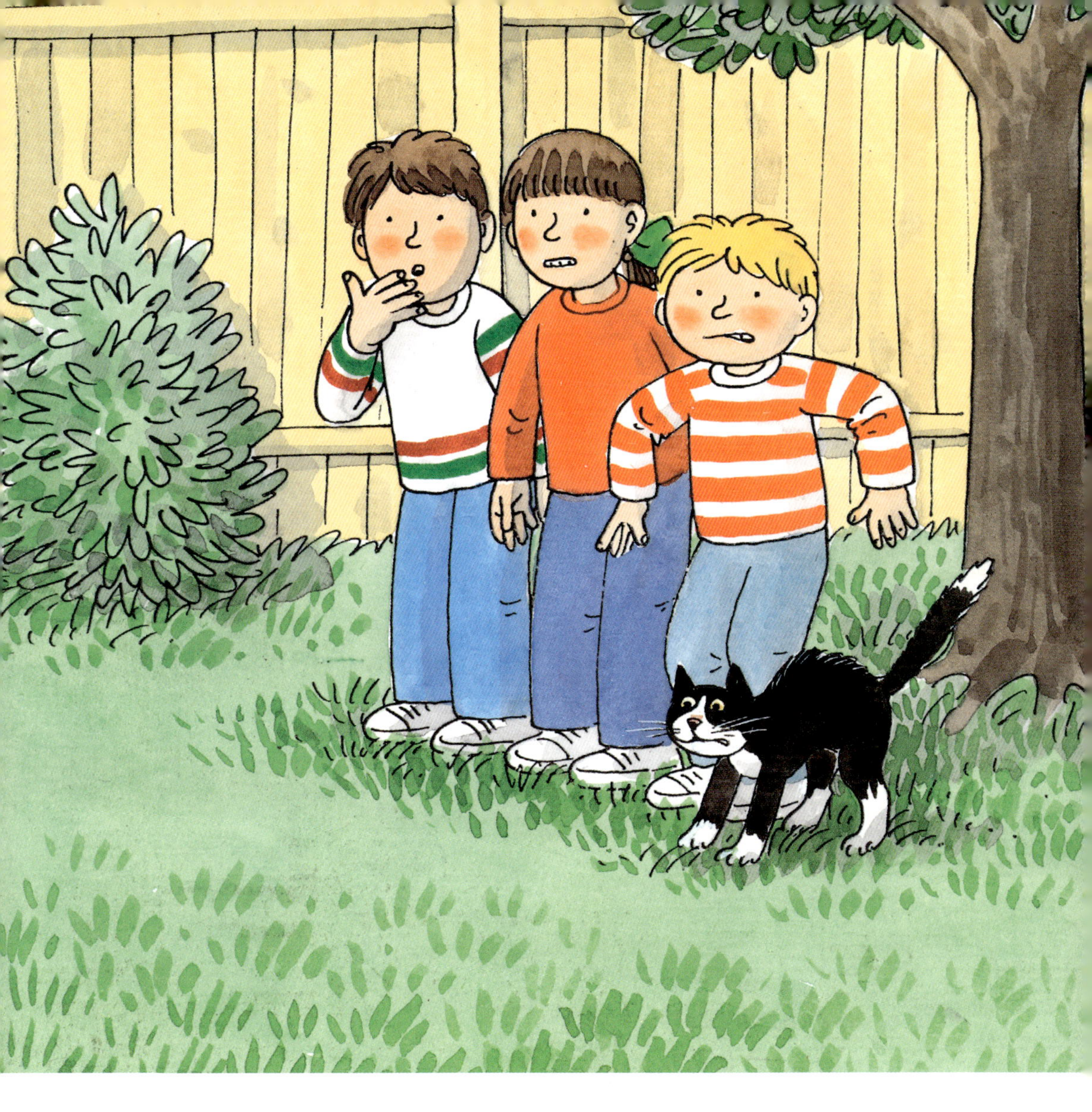

Floppy is coming.

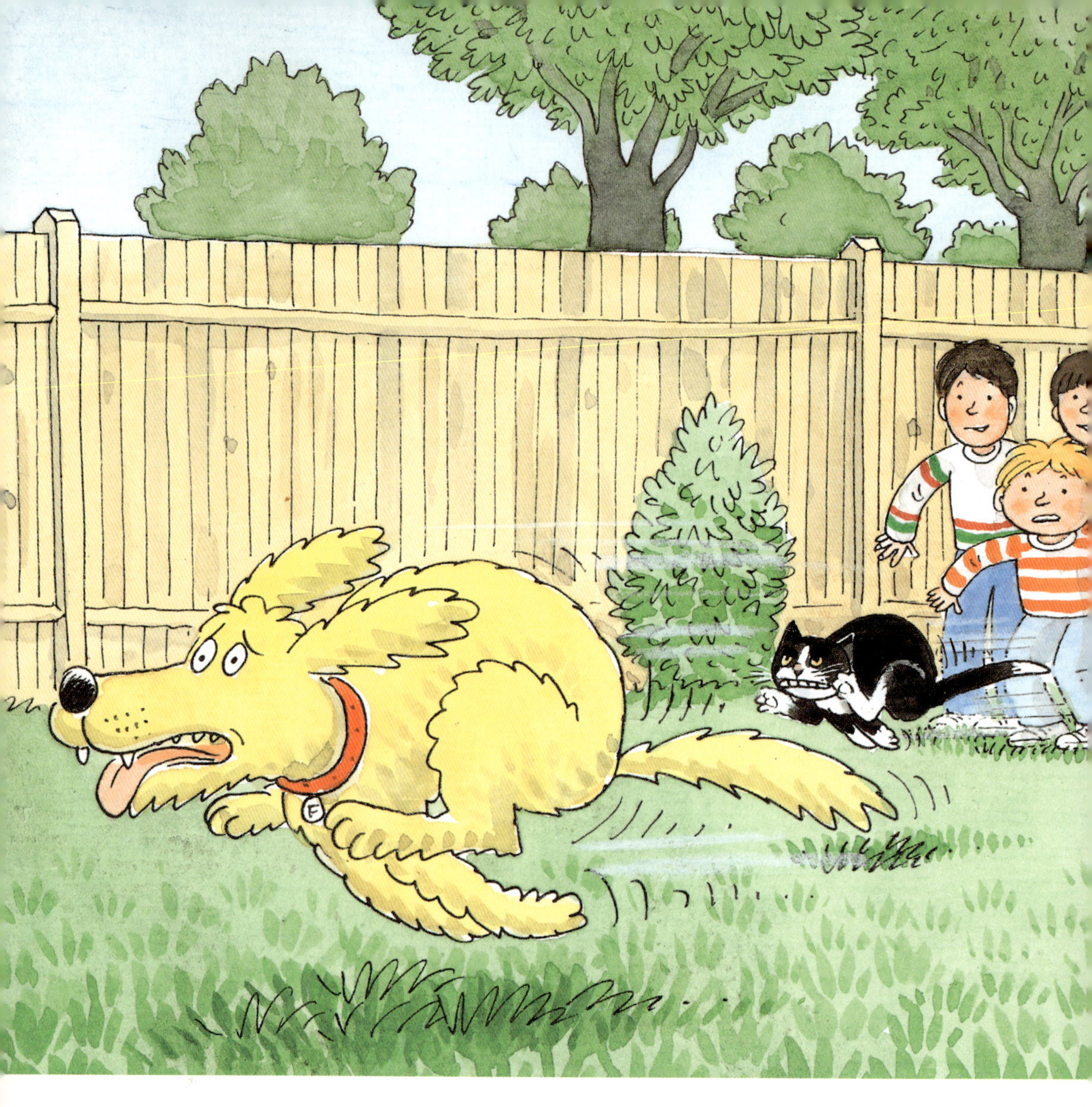

Oh, no!